Left Alone

Finding Strength for Life's Mysteries,
Impossibilities, and Uncertainties

By Ralph Douglas West

Left Alone

*Finding Strength for Life's Mysteries,
Impossibilities, and Uncertainties*

By Ralph Douglas West

Unless otherwise indicated, Scripture is taken from the New King James Version of the Bible.

Editing and layout: Pat Russo, http://web.mac.com/pgrusso/
Cover design: Worship Through the Arts,
www.worshipthroughthearts.com

© 2008 by Ralph Douglas West

ISBN 978-0-615-21569-3

Printed in the United States of America

To my pastors

Who are now part of the great cloud of witnesses:

Rev. O.C. Johnson, Sr., from Lyons Unity Missionary Baptist Church in Houston, Texas, who inspired my passion to preach.

Rev. Floyd D. Harris, Dallas, Texas, who taught me what it means to be a pastor.

Acknowledgements

This book was initially one big sermon designed to encourage an audience of preachers. As the content continued expanding, I thought that perhaps I had two separate messages.

The idea of putting those ideas into a book was not my idea. My preaching assistant and campus colleague Joel Gregory challenged me to assemble those messages into this printed format. It was Joel who saw that they would be helpful to people negotiating the intersections of life. Thanks Joel.

I also want to thank my loving congregation, the many folks who listen to me grapple weekly with the spiritual matters that scratch them where they itch. For twenty years, they have provided a dynamic and inviting atmosphere to preach and teach about the Kingdom of God.

My staff deserves my gratitude for keeping The Church Without Walls going on a daily basis. Their committed support enables me to be productive and makes this church the exciting place that it is.

Thank you to my assistant Consuella for your great work in managing my schedule, providing me with the freedom to efficiently execute my pastoral responsibilities.

An enormous thank you to my wife, Ree, for being the Rock of Gibraltar in our family. She exemplifies what it means to be "an ever present help." Her counsel and her suggestions improve upon every chapter that I write and every sermon that I preach.

The biggest thanks are reserved for my Lord, for calling me into His service as a Herald of His Word.

Sole Deo Gloria,

Ralph Douglas West

Table of Contents

Introduction

They weren't like any pictures or paintings that I'd ever seen. The first one I encountered was titled, "Kissing Cups" and the rendering so captured my imagination that I began seeking out similar artwork.

What fascinated me was that I had to look at these pictures — known as anamorphic illusions — in just the right way. Sometimes, that meant changing my approach or varying the angle from which I viewed them. At other times, it involved staring at the picture until my perspective was altered.

When the old woman's face melted away to reveal the portrait of a young woman staring into a mirror or the cups were transformed into another image, I always felt amply rewarded. It was all a matter of having the right perspective.

Anamorphic illusions are more than visual slights of hand. They suggest important lessons about how we can approach the mysterious periods in our lives, those times of uncertainty that test our faith, those long periods when we endure an impossible situation, those times when we feel that our souls are locked away in an isolation chamber. It's during these times that we need a different perspective.

By examining difficult times in the lives of Abraham, Elijah, and our Lord's disciples from a new direction, I hope to provide us with new angles and approaches that offer pathways leading out of these dark forests.

Ways to Use This Book

I'd like to suggest a few ways for you to approach this material:

As a devotional. Consider using each of these four chapters as the focus of your personal devotion for a week. Meditate on the Scripture verses, asking the Holy Spirit for insights into your personal situation. It might be helpful to use a journal to record your thoughts about and answers to the questions at the end of each chapter.

As material for group discussion. Each week, a Sunday school class or study group can examine a new chapter, using the chapter questions to promote discussion and further study.

As lessons within a Bible study. If you're planning or participating in a Bible study, think about incorporating this information into topical lessons dealing with life's difficulties.

Each of us encounters challenging times, days filled with pressing problems that we cannot unravel and painful puzzles that we cannot solve. It's my hope that this small book can help you to change your vantage point, helping you to again discover the hand of the Master on the canvas of your life.

All is mystery; but he is a slave who will not struggle to penetrate the dark veil.

— Benjamin Disraeli

God brings men into deep waters not to drown them, but to cleanse them.

— John H. Aughey

Chapter One — Left Alone in a Mystery
Genesis 22:1-8, 19

The story of Travis Walton's alleged abduction by aliens
sounds like something straight out of "The Twilight Zone."

On November 5, 1975, Travis was part of a seven-man crew
clearing trees on a government contract in the Arizona Apache-
Sitgreaves National Forest. At the end of the workday, the
crew jumped into a pick-up truck and began their trip home.
As they drove, they were shocked to see a "luminous object
shaped like a flattened disc" hovering on one side of the road.
Travis — still young and fearless — was enthralled by the
object's presence and left the truck to get a better look, against
the better wishes of his crewmates. As he gazed in wonder at
this object, a blue beam hit him, throwing him to the earth.
Understandably frightened, the six other men roared away in
the truck. Then, realizing that they had left Travis behind and
he might need help, they turned the truck around and headed
back to find him. When they returned to where they'd left him,
Travis Walton was gone.

After an unsuccessful search, the crew reported Travis'
disappearance to the police, launching the largest manhunt in
Arizona's history. Once word leaked out, this small Arizona

town was literally overrun by researchers, newspaper reporters, UFO buffs, and other curiosity seekers. After several days and no luck, the police began considering who might have a motive to murder Travis.

The men who were with Travis passed a series of polygraph examinations and days of interrogation by the police. That left only one other option — that their story was true. Then, five days after his disappearance, Travis Walton was found — feeble, hungry and dirty — lying on the cold pavement west of Heber, Arizona.

After his reappearance, Travis gave the following statement: "It was many years ago that I got out of a crew truck in the national forest and ran towards a glowing UFO hovering in the darkening Arizona sky. But when I made that fateful choice to leave the truck, I was leaving behind

Sometimes, we are left alone in a mystery that we cannot explain.

more than just my six fellow workmen. I was leaving behind forever all semblance of a normal life, running headlong toward an experience so overwhelmingly mind-rending in its effects, so devastating in its aftermath, that my life would never — could never — be the same again."

Travis was clearly alone. He had been left alone by his crewmates, left alone by the aliens who abducted him and left alone to face the aftermath of this strange experience. His story clearly reminds us that there is nothing as disconcerting as being left alone in the face of a mystery.

It's probably safe to say that you've never been abducted in a spaceship. It's likely also safe to assume that you know what it means to be left alone. Maybe the people you have trusted have left you. Some spouses have heard the words of separation — "I don't have anything left for you." Then, out the door they go, without a word of explanation.

Some children have experienced what it's like to be torn away from the comfort of home by the carelessness of a parent who puts a career ahead of the welfare of their children. Still others have discovered what it's like to be alone in some physical or emotional crisis, one that casts an elongated shadow across the horizon of their life.

Those of us in these situations can find guidance in Scripture. Genesis tells us the story about two nameless servants of Abraham. These two people were left alone in the midst of a spiritual crisis. From that solitary situation, they learned an important lesson that we all must learn. They learned the lesson of Divine trust.

It's a fact of life: *Sometimes we are left alone within a mystery that we cannot explain.*

When we find ourselves lost and alone within a mystery, we must realize that God is stretching our faith. We must realize that He wants us to draw nearer to Him in confident trust.

When we find ourselves left alone within a mystery, there are four things that can prove helpful. When we're left alone in a mystery, we must:

- Follow God faithfully
- Follow the leader loyally
- Wait patiently
- Believe deeply

Follow God faithfully
Imagine the eyewitness account of these two nameless servants of Abraham, two servants who watched their faithful leader follow God obediently for decades. They were part of the company of more than 100 servants who served and supported Abraham. They remembered God calling Abraham to leave Mesopotamia to pioneer a new frontier. They watched Abraham leave his father's house and venture with God — not knowing where he was going. All he had was the promise of this invisible God that called him.

They recalled Abraham reporting the promise God made to him concerning his future. God guaranteed that the name of Abraham would be great. And God also promised Abraham that his seed would be innumerable. What impressed the servants of Abraham the most about his new relationship with God was how he followed God without question. Abraham followed God without knowing where, waited on God without knowing when, and believed God without knowing how. He was a rock of faith.

But on one particular day, there was something different about the whole experience. Sarah watched as Abraham and Isaac left the house. For some unknown reason, she grieved quietly as her husband and her son walked toward the servants. She wept silently as only a mother can weep for her children. As Abraham and Isaac passed the large contingent of servants, they bowed their heads in silence. Although Abraham didn't say a word to them, they had been with him long enough to read his gestures. Abraham collected the wood himself. He called for the donkeys to be brought to him and grabbed his machete. He had nearly all of the accoutrements necessary for a sacrifice. But there was one obvious item that was missing — the sacrifice itself. Where was the sacrificial lamb?

We must realize that God is stretching our faith.

There was no time to wonder. At the words, "Let's go," the two servants broke camp and departed with Abraham, without being given any real explanation. When Abraham, Isaac, and the servants reached the base of the mountain, Abraham instructed the servants to stay behind while he and Isaac — his only son, whom he loved — went up the mountain to make a sacrifice and worship God. The servants were to remain until they returned.

The servants were left alone in a mystery. All they could do was to follow God as Abraham followed Him. The same confident demeanor that lived within Abraham had been passed on to his servants. These loyal servants mimicked the life of faith in God that was exemplified by Abraham. Like their master, they also followed God faithfully, even though they were facing a mystery without an explanation. They had to follow God faithfully while remaining stationary. This was one of the most difficult things they would have to do.

What about us? How faithfully do we follow God when we're facing a spiritual crisis? Recently, the secret letters of Mother Teresa were published. These letters have disclosed a side of Mother Teresa that has stimulated a series of debates among religionists, agnostics, and atheists concerning the validity of faith and doubt.

Mother Teresa — the "Saint of the Gutters" — spent her life as a missionary of mercy. She fed the hungry and gave refuge to the homeless. She studied medicine to better understand how to properly administer medication to the sick. She cradled the dying in her small, loving arms. But most of all, she pledged her life to Christ and took Him as her spouse.

Her letters reveal that for the last 50 years of her life, Mother Teresa endured a "dark night of the soul." She wrote the following letter to her confessor and confidant, the Rev. Michael Van der Peet. "Jesus has a very special love for you. But as for me, the silence and the emptiness

We have to follow God faithfully when we can't hear, feel, or even sense Him.

is so great, that I look and do not see, listen and do not hear — the tongue moves in prayer but does not speak...I want you to pray for me — that I let Him have His free hand."

In another letter, Mother Teresa feared that she would be a Judas to Jesus. Starting in the early 1960s, she found ways to live with this spiritual emptiness without abandoning either her belief or her work. Mother Teresa did not write one letter hinting at the possibility of reneging on her commitment of fidelity to her Lord. As Mother Teresa neared death, she wrote, *"If this brings You glory — if souls are brought to you — with joy, I accept all to the end of my life."*

Our greatest test is to follow God faithfully. We must follow God faithfully when we can't hear, feel, or sense Him. The real test of our love for God is revealed only as we follow Him despite our disappointment. We must each answer the question, "Will I stop serving God because of the gravity of the test?" Mother Teresa is not alone in feeling abandoned in a mystery. The saints of the ages have felt the same at times. The

Psalmist cries out, "Where is God in all of this?" The absence of His presence is a reality of faith. Faith that always sees and knows is not faith at all.

Follow the leader loyally
Before Abraham and Isaac began climbing the mountain, Abraham instructed his servants to remain at its base. The servants likely riveted their attention on Abraham, just as they had done so many times in the past. Their confidence was not misplaced.

These men had followed Abraham in and out of some tight places. They had followed Abraham from Haran to Canaan, they followed him off the beaten path to Egypt, and they watched as Abraham negotiated the labyrinth of famine. They followed Abraham when he pitched tents, built altars and prayed to God. They followed him when he made the difficult decision to let his nephew Lot journey to the lush plains of Sodom. And they remembered how Abraham labored and how he interceded for Lot's deliverance from Sodom and Gomorrah.

On two occasions, they remembered the poor choices he made in risking the chastity of Sarah to spare his own life. And still, they followed him. They followed him when Abraham and Sarah made the choice to get ahead of God. They followed him as the saga of Hagar and Sarah was an on-going source of tension. They were present for the birth of Ishmael, the protracted birth of Isaac, and the bitter debate between Abraham, Sarah, and Hagar about who was really Abraham's first born. They followed as Ishmael grew into a "wild ass man." And because these servants loved the whole clan, their hearts broke when Hagar and Ishmael had to strike camp and head toward the desert.

On this particular morning, these two servants didn't put any questions to Abraham. They hadn't questioned Abraham in the past, so there was no questioning his leadership now. If anyone had a right to raise questions, it was these two servants. Even in the tense moments of silence that morning, they didn't question Abraham. The lack of questions doesn't mean that they followed Abraham incredulously. They were instinctively aware of a paramount truth: Sometimes, questions are not appropriate.

In the earliest days of the telegraph, an unexpected phenomenon was revealed to telegraph operators in the American West. Along the endless stretches of wires, the vibration of one wire would sometimes be picked up by another wire running parallel on the same primitive pole. We call it sympathetic vibration: one wire being affected by the oscillations of another. In much the same way, Abraham's servants were sensing the same things that their master felt and reacting accordingly.

Leaders lead. No follower agrees with all the places that a
leader takes them. A true leader is tuned into a different
frequency. They live by rhythms that are not heard by others.
They can feel vibrations that others cannot detect. They listen
to the noise of silence. Leaders are peculiar. In reality, it takes a
good amount of trust in God — as well as in a leader — to
believe that they know where they're going.

Questions abound and a good leader listens. It's often the
questions of followers that stimulate good leaders. Any leader
worth his or her salt welcomes the questions that are put to
them. But there is a time for questioning and a time when those
questions must be silenced. Sometimes, you must follow the
leader in loyalty.

Ernest Shackleton's expedition on the Endurance was a result
of his determination to be the first to cross the Antarctic by foot
and claim the last prize in polar exploration for Britain. On
August 1, 1914 — one week after World War I began —
Shackleton and his diverse crew of twenty-seven men set sail
on the Endurance. They were not heard from again for nearly
two years.

For Shackleton and the crew, it was a particularly cold winter.
The pack ice of the Weddell Sea extended further north than
anyone could remember. The Endurance began navigating
through the pack ice on route to an intended landfall. On

January 10, 1915, just one day's sail from the Antarctic continent, temperatures plummeted and the ship became trapped, frozen in the ice for ten months. These conditions tested the leadership of Shackleton. Because the ice pressure was crushing the Endurance, Shackleton decided to abandon the ship.

For five months, the crew camped on drifting floes of ice. When open water appeared, they sailed three lifeboats through stormy seas to a rocky, uninhabited outcropping called Elephant Island. Knowing that his men would never survive on this desolate spot, Shackleton decided to attempt an incredible seventeen-day, 800-mile journey in freezing hurricane conditions. Taking one lifeboat, Shackleton and two of his men headed to the nearest civilization — South Georgia Island. The

Faith that always sees and knows is not faith at all.

lifeboat miraculously landed on the island, achieving what is now considered one of history's greatest boat journeys. Once on land, Shackleton and his men trekked across the mountains of South Georgia and reached the island's remote whaling stations. There, they organized a rescue team. On August 30, 1916, Shackleton returned to save the remainder of his crew, the men who had been left alone on Elephant Island.

This challenging adventure compels us to ask the question: Can we follow the leader loyally? To follow loyally, we must

believe in the person who is leading. Following loyally
involves praying for the person who is leading. But most of all,
following loyally means believing the one who leads is
following God.

There is a simple but profound formula for following a leader:
pray, pause, push.

•   Pray about following and ask God to validate what you
        see and hear.
•   Pause after the prayer to listen.
•   Then push forward with that leader.

Wait patiently
Genesis tells us that Abraham told his servants, "Stay here with
the donkey. The boy and I will travel a little farther. We will
worship there, and then we will come right back."

These two servants learned about waiting from Abraham. Long
before he requested this time of patience from his servants, he
modeled this quality for them. They knew exactly what waiting
meant because they served Abraham while he waited twenty-
five years for Isaac. They also knew that most of the trouble
that Abraham found himself in had something to do with his
inability to wait.

As they waited, these two servants were fulfilling what the
military calls "general orders," which means staying at your

post until someone comes to relieve you. The general orders of the Army, the Air Force, the Marine Corps and the Navy are the same: I will guard everything within the limits of my post and quit my post only when properly relieved.

On December 26, 1944, Hiroo Onoda was sent to Lubang Island in the Philippines, approximately seventy-five miles southwest of Manila, to lead a garrison in guerilla warfare. Shortly after American forces landed, all but four of the Japanese soldiers in his command either died or surrendered.

Unaware that the war ended on August 15, 1945, Hiroo Onoda and the other Japanese soldiers were left alone on the island for decades. Over time, the other men died. Onoda refused every suggestion and every attempt to convince him that the war was over, seeing every encounter as a ruse or a trap to get him to desert his post. Despite the letters and newspapers left for him, the radio broadcasts, and even family pleas, Onoda would not face the fact that he was abandoned and left alone. He remained at his post for many years to come.

On February 20, 1973, Onoda encountered a young Japanese university dropout who questioned his loyalty to forces that no longer existed. Onoda stated that he would remain at his post until he received orders from one of his commanders. Feeling obligated to help Onoda, the student returned to Japan and located the soldier's one-time superior, Major Yoshimi

Taniguchi. Twenty-nine years after WWII ended, Onoda received his orders and emerged from the jungle in his dress uniform and sword. His Arisake Type 99 rifle was still in operating condition and he still had 500 rounds of ammunition and several grenades. He was declared a national hero in Japan just because he waited. Many times you can be a spiritual hero just because you wait.

So much of what we do in life is waiting. Experts estimate that

Whenever waiting is involved, there is always a temptation to quit.

during a 70-year lifetime, Americans spend three to five years just waiting. While technology has added conveniences to our lives, it has created new wait times. Consider that the average computer user spends nine minutes per day simply waiting for downloads.

It takes an incredible amount of patience and commitment to wait, to faithfully remain at your post. Some of you have been waiting for years for prayers to be answered. Others have been waiting patiently for a job, a marriage, or a ministry circumstance to improve. Without a doubt, remaining patient has been the most difficult part of this task.

Whenever waiting is involved, there is always a temptation to quit. We find ourselves fatalistically thinking, "This is my lot in life. Things are just not going to get any better."

When we feel like this, it takes every ounce of self-control we have to simply continue to stand at our posts. We may have been with the Lord for years and witnessed God's activity in other people's lives. Rather than listening to those doubts, we must remind ourselves that we cannot quit; we must keep waiting. Let me encourage you to continue waiting. Remember that Scripture tells us, "They that wait on the Lord shall renew their strength."[1]

Believe deeply

On top of the mountain, Abraham had to offer to God the most precious gift he had ever received. He took his son, his only son Isaac — whom he loved — and offered him back to God. Soren Kierkegaard is right; before faith we experience dread. In spite of his momentary dread, we can see that Abraham loved God. We know this because he willingly gave back to God what ultimately did not belong to him.

Before Abraham left his servants alone in a mystery, he said that he was taking Isaac to worship God. In faith, he also said that God would provide the lamb for the sacrifice. Abraham was ready to sacrifice to God; we know this because he carried with him the necessary wood, the rope, the fire, and the knife. Only when he saw these elements did Isaac ask his father, "Where is the lamb for the sacrifice?" Abraham answered him, "The Lord will provide."

On the mountain, we are introduced to a new way of
identifying the person and presence of God. He is the God of

**We never know
how deeply we
believe in God
until we face an
unbelieveable
crisis.**

prevision and of *provision*. In His
prevision, God sees what we need. In
His provision, God gives us the
things that we need. While Abraham
needed a substitute sacrifice, there
was no indication that one would be
granted. Still Abraham's faith was not
deterred. With his hand raised, he wielded the knife to take the
life of his son.

Suddenly, he heard the bleating of a ram caught in the thicket.
Miraculously and dramatically, God provided. Abraham and
Isaac successfully worshiped God on the mountain. Then they
prepared to return and relieve the two waiting servants.

Abraham's faith had deepened. Isaac's faith had deepened.
Each servant's faith had deepened. Hopefully, our faith is also
deepening. Great tests are often used to mature us as believers.
We will never know how deeply we believe in God until we
have faced an unbelievable crisis.

Reflect over your life. Recall those times when you have
believed deeply. You didn't believe deeply on the mountain; it
was in the valley that you began to believe deeply. You didn't
believe deeply during the spring of life, but in the midst of the

icy winter. You didn't believe deeply at birth, only in death.

In this life, when we are left alone in a mystery, we must remember that we are experiencing a lesson in Divine trust. We must remind ourselves that it's important for our faith to be exercised; we must realize the importance of drawing near to God in confident trust. As our faith matures, this lesson of Divine trust is one that we will appreciate more and more deeply.

In the midst of the ravages of World War II, when hundreds of thousands lived with the daily threat of starvation, a single mother was left alone to provide for her children. The meals were slight, the food was sparse, and the children lived on the edge. Sensing their anxiety, the mother placed a tin box on top of the family icebox. Many times, she pointed to the box and told the children, "If worse comes to worse, we can always open the box." The little children were too short to reach the box, but they always wondered what was in it.

After the war, the oldest son brought the adult children together when their mother passed. They gathered around the icebox once again, looking at the ancient tin breadbox. As the oldest son opened the box, he passed it to the others. Each one saw that there was nothing in it. Their mother had pointed to an empty box in order to give them hope.

Like these children, we must confront the empty aspects of our faith. We face an empty altar, an empty cross, and an empty tomb. But this emptiness is not meaningless. We have emptiness only because the Savior departed. The altar was only empty until God provided. The tomb was empty because God provided. And the cross is empty because He came down in order to go up.

Our hope is not based on empty promises. Just as Abraham faced an empty altar, we too look at empty places and wait for God to provide. Instead of empty altars, we struggle against empty homes, empty bank accounts and empty hearts. Instead of empty tombs, we daily live with empty beds, empty futures and empty plans.

In the midst of this, our Savior tells us to be of good cheer. In the midst of a mystery — in the twinkling of an eye — God can fill that emptiness. There is always a ram and always a Lamb; just look around you.

Somewhere nearby, God is filling the emptiness. He filled an altar with a ram. He filled a widow's jars with oil. He filled stone pots with wine. He filled 5,000 with bread and fish.

It's there for you right now. Push through the mystery and God will provide.

References

1. Isaiah 40:31

Reflection Questions

Suggested readings: Genesis 22 and Hebrews 11:8-19

1. Recall a time when you struggled with a mystery. What do you remember thinking and feeling?

2. Our biggest challenge during these situations is to continue following God in faith. What made it difficult for you to follow God faithfully? How did you get past this challenge?

3. Have you ever followed a leader loyally despite questions and concerns? Was your faith rewarded? If not, were you able to successfully deal with the disappointment?

4. Have you ever believed deeply despite trying situations and circumstances? What was the outcome of your faith? How has this affected you during other times of testing?

5. Do you find it difficult to be patient in trying circumstances? Is it challenging for you to overcome negative thinking during these times? What might you do differently?

6. How has God stretched your faith through the situations you have faced? How might you apply this knowledge to a mystery that you are currently facing?

Character cannot be developed in ease and quiet. Only through experiences of trial and suffering can the soul be strengthened, vision cleared, ambition inspired and success achieved.

—— Helen Keller

Difficulties show men what they are. In case of any difficulty, remember that God has pitted you against a rough antagonist that you may be a conqueror, and this cannot be without toil.

—— Epictetus

Chapter Two — Left Alone in an Impossibility
Mark 5:21-24, 35-42; 9:1-29; 14:32-42

They may be the world's most beautiful doors.

Ten panels that illustrate scenes from the immortal poems of Robert Browning, the 19th century British poet, are cast into the massive bronze doors that grace the front of the Armstrong Browning Library at Baylor University in Waco, Texas.

The treasures inside the library far surpass the entry doors. Astonishing stained glass windows vie for attention with Browning's personal autographs, sculptures commissioned by the family, and even a lock of the poet's hair. Yet everyday, some choose to remain outside the library, staying beyond the reach of the astonishing wonders awaiting them.

While some may take pains to avoid outstanding educational experiences, others find it difficult to remain alert while on the edge of action. In February 2008, a startling commercial aviation snafu nearly caused a disaster. For nearly a half hour, air traffic controllers were unable to contact the pilot and the co-pilot of a plane heading to Hawaii after it flew past the destination stated on its flight plan. At a critical moment, both men had fallen asleep at the wheel.

Even though some people will forever choose to remain outside and others will slumber contentedly, we will still be graced by the presence of heroes and heroines. Some of them may live nearby, even in our towns and in our neighborhoods. Still others may be seated nearby during Sunday morning worship. Some of these brave folks will become heroes and heroines who belong to the ages.

While we may or may not recognize their names, it's what they've done that has set them apart for ages to come. There

All of us are sometimes locked out of promising situations.

may be a teacher who's taken a special interest in a student from a troubled home. There may be a cafeteria worker who made sure that a hungry child had a meal to eat. There may be someone who simply acted as a surrogate father or mother to a young person who's a long way from home.

If you inquire further, you'll find something that may surprise you: Much of the time, these folks didn't feel like heroes at all. Most felt exactly the opposite. They've felt locked out of what was really going on on the other side. They've been left to struggle through a situation while others get the glory. Sometimes, they've been too tired to keep up and are forced to the edge of what could have been a promising situation.

If you were to sit down with any of the heroes who have been preserved for the ages, they'd tell you that none of their achievements have come without some amount of difficulty. That's true for everyone. Regardless of who we are, all of us come face-to-face with impossibilities. All of us are sometimes locked out of promising situations, abandoned at the bottom of a mountain of difficulties, or nearly overcome with weariness on the edge of the action.

Military history has no shortage of people who have felt locked out and left behind. Even brave, vigilant soldiers are left behind in some difficult-to-explain impossibilities. When President Franklin Roosevelt commanded General Douglas MacArthur to leave the Philippines in 1942 for Melbourne, Australia, it was the most difficult order MacArthur had been asked to follow. MacArthur knew that he would be leaving thousands of faithful soldiers who had served with him for years. And yet, these orders had to be obeyed.

When the Japanese captured the Philippines, 72,000 US soldiers were taken prisoner and forced into the Bataan death march, one of the worst war crimes in history. These soldiers were marched for sixty miles to a concentration camp, often without food and water. During the march, 18,000 died. Some were executed during the march, while others died from malaria, starvation or dehydration. Another 30,000 died at the hands of their captors, many after being tortured.

When word of this atrocity reached MacArthur, it was the darkest day of his life. He felt responsible for the many men who were killed. The few soldiers who survived said that they held onto one hope for survival. Before MacArthur left the island, he gave them his promise, "I shall return."

I wish that I could tell you that you'll get through life without difficulty. You don't have to look for problems, you don't have to sign up for them, or solicit them. They just have a way of finding you. Even when you turn your attention in another direction, difficulties and impossibilities of one kind or another are always staring you right in the face.

What can you do when you find yourself left alone and facing the impossible? How do you function? When you're facing the impossible, when you're in the midst of some circumstance beyond your control, remember this one important fact: God specializes in the impossible. Our God can do what no other power can do.

The Gospel of Mark gives us three neatly woven stories that offer tools and insights for those times when we're facing the impossible. We'll look specifically at times when we're left alone:

- On the other side of a locked door
- At the bottom of a mountain
- In the corner of a garden

On the other side of a locked door
Some are standing in front of a locked door today, facing an impossible situation. This was certainly the case with Jairus, a story that's described in Mark 5.

As a leader of the Sanhedrin, Jairus didn't believe in a future bodily resurrection. That changed when his twelve-year-old daughter became deathly ill and he needed help from the other side of the door. Jairus set those beliefs aside and went searching for Jesus. He knew that his only option was to appeal to the mercy and the sensibilities of Jesus, to ask Him to break away from His busy ministry schedule and heal his daughter.

"My daughter," Jairus said, "is sick to the point of death. Could you come and help?" Without any further discussion, Jesus agreed. Even before Jesus began walking toward his home, Jairus must have seen the messenger coming his way. "Don't bother the teacher any longer," the messenger told him. "Your daughter is dead."

As the announcement of his daughter's death began to sink in, Jairus was quickly faced with an important decision. Looking directly at him, Jesus asked, "Do you believe?" Then, turning to leave the crowd behind, Jesus and Jairus headed toward the shaken man's home.

When they arrived at the house, it was already filled with attendants singing funeral dirges and mourners draped in their death garb. When Jesus announced that the girl was only sleeping, the mourning was transformed into mocking as they ridiculed our Lord. Then Jesus firmly put the people out of the house and closed the doors behind them. The only ones allowed to witness this miracle were the disciples and Jairus. They saw Jesus call to the girl and awaken her.

In the moment of seeking, we find. And in the very act of knocking, we find.

It was their unbelief that prevented these people from seeing what was on the other side of the locked door. Their faithless perspective kept them from moving forward. They were left alone to face the impossibility of death.

We can learn an important lesson from this story: When we're shut out, we should stand and wait faithfully until our answer comes from the other side.

A famous story about someone needing a blessing from the other side of a locked door occurred in January of 1077 and involved Henry IV. Before he was deposed and excommunicated by Pope Gregory, Henry had been the Holy Roman Emperor, the most powerful political figure in the world. He waited two months for the pope to send word that he'd been readmitted to the church, but no message arrived. Two months later, Henry appeared at Canossa, an impregnable fortress on the northern slope of the Apennines.

Intent on begging the pope to restore him to the church, the emperor stood from the twenty-fifth to the twenty-eighth of January in the court between the inner walls as a penitent, with a bare head and bare feet. The winter of 1077 was one of the coldest recorded in history. For three days, Henry knocked in vain for entrance.

Remember that Jesus often stands just on the other side of a locked door.

The stern old pope, as hard as rock and cold as snow, refused his entrance. The sight of this fallen ruler was said to be so pitiful that people wept when they saw him. When the inner gate was finally opened, the deposed king entered to receive what he needed from the other side.

Isn't this story remarkably similar to something that Jesus told us? When we can't see what's on the other side of that locked door, keep asking, keep seeking and keep knocking until the answer comes. Jesus promises that we receive even as we open our mouths to ask, that in the very moment of seeking we find, and in the very act of knocking we find an opening.

Maybe you're standing before a locked door today. You may be waiting for the doctor to bring you good news. You may be waiting for a verdict to be passed down by a jury. You may be

When we're shut out, we should stand faithfully until our answer comes from the other side.

waiting for an admission committee to open the door of a college. You may be waiting for the HR department to hire you. You may even be waiting for a prodigal child to return from a faraway land. As you wait, remember that Jesus often stands just on the other side of a closed door.

The story of Jairus' daughter is a reminder that faith is the key to unlocking the door. If you are waiting today for something good to come from the other side, be patient and wait in faith for the answer. Remember the question that Jesus asked: "Do you believe?"

Facing the mountains of impossibility
At times, it feels that we are alone at the bottom of a mountain and cannot do anything. In Mark 9, we find a story about this type of situation.

Jesus left nine disciples at the base of the mountain to serve the multitude that followed Him, taking Peter, James and John to the top of the mountain. These three disciples were witnesses to Jesus' transfiguration and then had to return to the base camp. On the mountain, they saw Jesus in resplendent glory. They were so overjoyed that they exclaimed, "Let's stay here and build three tabernacles." They wanted to honor Jesus and his guests, Moses and Elijah. But they soon learned that the top of the mountain is a No Parking Zone. They could not remain on the summit; it was only a place for them to be refueled, replenished and refreshed. They had to return to the "B team" that was serving the crowds down below.

Upon their arrival, they encountered a curious disturbance. They met a father with a chronically ill son who the nine disciples could not heal. Both the father and the disciples were disturbed, since none of them could figure out why their prayers were not working.

Seeing Jesus, the father immediately began explaining the situation. He told the Savior how his boy continued cutting himself, throwing himself in the fire, or trying to drown or strangle himself.

Turning toward His disciples, Jesus made some very pointed comments. "You faithless generation," He said. "How is it that you have been with me all this time, have seen me handle this same situation, yet you're puzzled and ineffective? Weren't you with me when a boy was healed of leprosy? Did you see me restore a man's legs and heal him of his sins after his friends lowered him through the roof? Weren't you there in the temple when the man's withered hand was straightened?"

"Do you remember how I hushed the winds, calmed the waves and quieted the waters? What about the exorcism in Gerasenes, the 12-year old girl who had been dead, and the feeding of the multitude with a few fish and some bread? If you remember all this, how is it that you still don't know how to serve in my name? It can only be because you do not believe!"

Turning to the father, Jesus asked, "Do you believe?" Challenged by what he had just heard, the man replied, "Lord, I believe, but help my unbelief." While he appeared to only possess a half-hearted faith, it was enough faith for Jesus to work with. It only takes a small portion of faith to move impossibilities. "If you have faith the size of a mustard seed, you can say to this mountain be moved and it will be done."[1]

Jesus doesn't require us to have lots of faith. If His disciples had remembered that, they could have handled the situation while the others were on top of the mountain. Even a small portion of faith is enough to work with. When Jesus encountered that faith in the father waiting in the base camp, He brought power from above to those who were powerless below.

At the bottom of the mountain, the disciples could not serve. They were powerless against the sickness that violently gripped this young boy. They were in the vice-like grip of impotent faith and the impossibilities loomed large in their presence.

When we're facing the mountain of impossibility and cannot serve, we must remember how desperately we need the power of God. "Apart from Me, you can do nothing,"[2] Jesus tells us. None of us can serve God in our own

Remember the question that Jesus asked, "Do you believe?"

strength and might. We need the power of God to help us in His service. We can't preach without God's power. We can't sing without God's power. We can't even witness without God's power.

In these situations, the only thing we can do is to wait — wait for power to come down from the mountain to deliver us from our powerlessness. When we are at the foot of the mountain in the base camp of impossibility, we must wait until the power from above comes down.

Twelve hundred years prior to this, there was a similar episode at the foot of another mountain. When Moses climbed Mt. Sinai to receive a message from the hand of God, he left Aaron to lead the children of Israel. Because he listened to the wrong voices at the bottom of the mountain, Aaron nearly sabotaged the future of Israel.

"Let's build a god," the voices told Aaron. "You can do it; you can fashion it from our image and your imagination." Aaron began collecting their golden earrings, their platinum, and their diamonds so he could begin crafting an image that was a violation of everything that God had revealed.

There are important lessons here. Whether we're left alone at the base of the mountain to serve or to lead, we must be careful about what we listen to and what we hear. The bottom of the

None of us can serve God in our own strength and might.

mountain is no place for us to be neutral. The Hippocratic Oath reminds every physician of his or her duties and

responsibilities. It tells them that if they cannot heal, they should cause no harm. Likewise, when we are left alone at the bottom of the mountain, we should cause no harm.

The bottom of the mountain is also not a place to lose hope. You may recognize Sir Edmund Hillary's name because of his famous ascent of Mt. Everest in 1953. What you might not know is that he wasn't originally supposed to be the only one to make this notable climb. When the other climbers became too weak, too tired or too cold to assault the peak, the job fell to Hillary and his Sherpa guide, Tinzang Norgay. The others had to remain at the bottom of the mountain while these two men went to the top.

But the question is not why we must wait at the bottom while others partake of the glory at the top. Instead, the question is whether we believe that Jesus is Lord of every lowly situation and is both ready and willing to act on our behalf.

Alone in a corner of the garden

In the garden at Sudeley Castle, many tall, sentinel-like yew trees form the walls of a maze at the edge of the garden. This garden, found in the midst of the picturesque English landscape, attracts visitors from around the globe. Every year, scores of tourists get lost in the labyrinth of the yew trees. It doesn't take long for a careless visitor to become trapped within the maze, lost just on the other side of the beautiful garden on the other side of these green walls. Sometimes, even faithful followers of Jesus feel lost at the edge of something beautiful and important.

After sharing the Passover with his disciples, Jesus had Calvary in full view. In Mark 14, He goes to the Garden of Gethsemane with His disciples. The name, "Gethsemane," tells us something about what happened there. The name itself means a pressing place, a place of pressure.

Jesus walked with the disciples to the garden and then asked them to stay behind, to wait for Him and to pray. Like the disciples, there will be times when we'll be left in the corner of the garden, times where we ought to stay alert and not go to sleep.

Jesus went on a bit further and prayed. When He returned to
His disciples and found them sleeping, He was disappointed.
"You couldn't watch with me one hour? You fell into
temptation and slipped into sleep." He encouraged them to
battle this temptation and went off to pray again.

Again, Jesus returned to find His disciples sleeping. They
weren't supporting Him by interceding, they weren't available
as He struggled in prayer, sweating drops of blood. They were
napping. Jesus roused them once again. "Wake up, friends. It's
not that late. You've been up later for fish fries in Galilee. Stay
alert and encourage one another to pray."

Again, Jesus goes off to pray and returns to finds His disciples
slumbering, knowing that His betrayal was approaching. We
cannot fault the disciples for their actions. There are many

**We need the
power of God to
help us in His
service.**

times when we should be attentive,
with our eyes riveted upon Heaven,
focusing on God to pray down the
redemptive possibilities for tomorrow
— and yet we're just not that

engaged. We wake up on Sunday morning, show up at church
and yet our spirits and our hearts are sometimes fast asleep.

We don't go to sleep at the movies and we don't go to sleep at
the birthday bashes. When it comes to the things of God, that's
when we miss it. Some of us are in need of a miracle. Some of

us are asking God for direction. We need the power of His possibilities to re-energize our lives and our ministries. And like the disciples in the garden, we often cannot find the strength to stay alert. We've become lost in the maze and may be ready to fall asleep on this side of significance. Yet, even when we're overwhelmed by a series of dead ends and cold trails, the vigilance and faithfulness of our Living Lord offers us the strength we need to remain awake, alert and watchful.

Like the disciples in the garden, we often cannot find the strength we need to stay alert.

John Grey was a police officer who lived in Edinburgh, Scotland in 1858. He had a constant companion named Bobby, who was a Scottish terrier. When John succumbed to tuberculosis, he was buried in the churchyard of the Greyfriars Cemetery. For the next fourteen years, that little Scottish terrier refused to leave his master's grave. The townspeople began calling the dog Bobby Greyfriars. Sometimes, they switched it around and referred to him as Greyfriars Bobby.

If you go to Edinburgh today, you'll see the statue that was erected in 1873 in honor of this loyal and faithful dog that stood watch over his master's grave. For fourteen years, the only time Bobby left the grave was for his one o'clock meal. He became so popular that the big hotels and restaurants would

set out delicate meals for him eat. He remained a faithful
companion for years, even after his master was dead.

When I consider Greyfriars Bobby, it challenges me. If a dog
can keep his eyes on his dead master for that long, how much

**God has a
solution for
anyone who
feels alone in
the face of
impossibilities.**
more should be expected from the
disciples of the Living Lord? We ought
to have at least that much faith and
confidence in God. Unlike Bobby's
master, our Master may return at any
moment to find us. We cannot afford to
be sleeping or to be unprepared. We

want our Lord to return to faithful, expectant servants who are
not dismayed by impossibilities because they are trusting in
Him.

Whether we're at the edge of the garden, at the bottom of the
mountain, or on the other side of a locked door, Christ can
come to us. He wants to find us believing; He wants to
repurpose and redirect our lives. Our failures don't matter to
Him. God has a solution for anyone who feels alone in the face
of impossibilities. He has strength for us and He has power for
us.

It doesn't matter if we have rivers that seem impossible to
cross or mountains that loom in our path. It doesn't matter if

we're facing an impossible sickness, emotional pain, or the death of a loved one. We can still maintain a good confession because of this fact: God specializes in fixing things that seem impossible. It might seem impossible to the human eye, but our God is a wonder worker.

Sometimes, God allows us to be put into impossible situations. He doesn't do this to hurt or to humiliate us; He does it to stretch our faith beyond its borders. He does it to let us know that He is Lord of the impossible. When He takes us through those impossible situations, we should give Him all the glory. When you are locked out, stuck at the bottom or lost within a maze, remember that God does honor simple faithfulness.

Peter, James and John — the inner circle of the disciples — went behind the door at the house of Jairus, on top of the mountain at the Transfiguration, and inside the Garden of Gethsemane with Jesus. The other disciples were left outside the door, at the bottom of the mountain and at the edge of the Garden. Yet they demonstrated faithfulness by waiting, by believing, and by standing by in cluelessness and drowsiness. They were still there, even in the midst of the bleakest night, obediently standing at the edge and not knowing what would come next.

We serve a faithful Lord. From either inside or outside the

door, He can say, "Behold, I stand at the door and knock." He may beckon you from inside to wait or from outside to enter.

All He requires is that we listen for His voice in the midst of our situations and at the edge of our challenges.

References

1. Matthew 17:20
2. John 15:5

Reflection Questions

Suggested readings: 1 Kings 19 and Hebrews 11:32-40

1. Has facing an impossible situation ever provided you with new insights about yourself? What actions or changes did this prompt you to take?

2. Have you ever felt trapped on the other side of a locked door? What made it difficult to wait faithfully for what you needed? What might you have done differently?

3. Do you believe that no significant character change comes without difficulty? How does this belief affect situations you are facing now or might face in the future?

4. Recall a situation where you were powerless that God changed for you. How has this experience changed the way that you've faced other impossible situations?

Uncertainty and mystery are energies of life. Don't let them scare you unduly, for they keep boredom at bay and spark creativity.
— *R. I. Fitzhenry*

Those who believe that they believe in God, but without passion in their hearts, without anguish in mind, without uncertainty, without doubt, without an element of despair even in their consolation, believe only in the God-Idea, not in God Himself.
— *Miguel de Unamuno*

Chapter Three — Left Alone in Uncertainty
1Kings 19

When Bishop James Pike was reported missing in the Judean Desert in 1969, the story got front-page coverage from *The New York Times*. A well-known, colorful figure in the Episcopal Church, Bishop Pike had been embroiled in a number of controversies over the years.

Raised a Roman Catholic, Pike became an agnostic while in college and went on to study law at Yale. During World War II, he found himself drawn to the Episcopal Church. After the war, Pike studied at Union Theological Seminary and began a priestly career that gave him a national reputation after he became the Episcopal bishop of the diocese of California.

Pike often used his pulpit to attack organized religion for its racial and political views, which resulted in him being branded as a dangerous radical by conservative Episcopalians. In 1966, he resigned his position with the church. Searching for a deeper meaning in Christianity, Pike and his wife Diane took a trip to Jerusalem in hopes of retracing the actual steps of Jesus. He set out from Bethlehem in a rented car on September 2, 1969, intending to reach the wilderness where Jesus was tempted by the devil. When the paved roads ended abruptly and the car was stuck in a rut, Pike abandoned his vehicle and began walking through the desert. His body was found a few days later by a search party.

Centuries earlier, another outspoken man of God headed into the desert. When the prophet Elijah entered the desert, he was

It is entirely possible for us to find springs of faith deep within our own desert of doubt. running, not walking. In his attempt to escape from evil, he had a life-changing encounter with God. Like Elijah, we can head into the desert feeling depleted and defeated and return replenished and renewed. We can walk through the desert of doubt and the wilderness of despair without dying. It is entirely possible for us to find springs of faith deep within our own desert of doubt.

Elijah remains one of the most significant characters in the Old Testament, second only to Moses. He appears in the Biblical record already fully grown and hailing from Tishba, an unknown place with an unrecorded address. He seemingly came from nowhere and departed in a chariot of fire. He was a spiritual giant, a champion of Israel, faithfully obeying God and executing his prophetic office. Elijah believed deeply and waited patiently on God at his assigned posts.

After Elijah's storied and famous triumph over the prophets of Baal on Mt. Carmel, he returned to the northern kingdom in power. That's when the villainous wife of King Ahab called him out and ordered him to leave the kingdom. When he learned that Queen Jezebel had placed a bounty on his head, Elijah panicked. In spite of his tremendous victory over the prophets of Baal and his miraculous ability to outrun the king's chariots, he felt both helpless and hopeless. Elijah went into the desert to retreat from his prophetic responsibilities.

Elijah wasn't the only person affected by his inability to overcome his desert of doubt. The troubled prophet also abandoned his servant at the edge of the desert, at the very southern border of the Holy Land, at what was considered the end of civilization. The nameless servant of Elijah points out some timeless truths; we can learn major lessons from this minor Old Testament character. It's significant that the experience of being left alone in the wilderness by his mentor did not destroy this young lad's faith in God or his respect for his mentor. This young man's life can teach us how to focus on our own faith journey when someone close to us runs from God.

It's never easy to be left alone. It doesn't matter if it's a mentor, a spouse, or a friend that's abandoned us. The reasons they give for leaving us and running from God are usually pretty difficult to swallow. Sometimes, these explanations don't even make sense. All we know is that we're left alone; whenever that happens, our own doubts begin finding much louder voices.

Regardless of the particulars of our situation, we can find victory over our doubts and emerge with our faith and our self-respect intact. The story of Elijah's servant offers us a number of useful principles that will help us to weather these solitary journeys.

When he was left alone, Elijah's servant did four things. He:

- Traveled as far as possible
- Remained faithful
- Trusted in a caring God
- Prepared to welcome Elijah back

Travel as far as possible

When Queen Jezebel threatened Elijah's life, it shattered his confidence. His faith was gone, he was defeated and he lost his assurance that Yahweh was God. He no longer believed that good would overcome evil. He was no longer focused on God's protection, only on what he could do to save himself. Turning to behaviors that helped him to survive in the past, he began relying upon his own desert expertise and his hard-won outdoor experience.

Everyone does this at times. When a sudden, unexpected crisis threatens us, our eyes are diverted from the power of Christ. We see only the threatening circumstances closing in around us. Our faith fails and we want to run for our lives.

This story also shows how Elijah's pride distanced him from
his servant. He wouldn't allow the young man to witness the
effect that the queen's threats were
having on him. That's why he only
allowed his servant to escort him as
far as Beersheba. Elijah didn't want
anyone — not even his own servant
— to see him in the desperate desert

**Elijah's faith was
gone, he was
defeated and lost
his assurance that
Yahweh was God.**

of his despondency. He didn't want anyone to witness his
personal failure or his humiliation. Planning to remain in
solitude, he instructed his young servant to stay behind.

It was difficult enough for Elijah to tuck tail and run in the face
of this woman's fury. He likely didn't want the added
responsibility of thinking about how his own struggle might
affect his servant's faith. It was easier to leave the young
servant and head into the desert alone. Zoology experts tell us
that when an elephant is mortally wounded, it goes off in the
wilderness to die. Instinctively, that's what Elijah was doing.

Elijah's servant did the only thing that he could do: he went as
far as his master permitted and stayed behind. Until his mentor
regained his confidence, the servant could only focus on caring
for himself. In those days, Beersheba was the end of
civilization. The lad — who some believe to be the widow's
son that Elijah brought back from the dead — had to stand at

his post until the prophet returned to claim him.

This young man had plenty of things to keep him occupied.
Nearby was Hebron, the very place where the patriarchs were
buried. Jutting out of the ground were the headstones of
Abraham, Sarah, Isaac, and Jacob. We can picture this young
man reading the epitaphs carved in the stone as a way of
refreshing himself. Surely, this helped him to rehearse the story
of God's faithfulness to his people, to his master Elijah, as well
as to himself.

Romans 12:18 tells us, "If it is possible, as far as it depends on
you, live at peace with everyone." We cannot hold ourselves
accountable for someone else's actions and decisions; we can
only do those things that depend on us. We must leave the rest
to God. There will be times when those who are important to
us will only permit us to journey to a certain point with them.
Like Elijah's servant, we can only execute our responsibility by
traveling to that point. Then, we must let them go into their
personal wilderness. We cannot always move forward with the
dear people we want to help. We have to release them to fight
their own battles.

After being defeated in the 1912 presidential election,
Theodore Roosevelt longed for one more adventure, a final
chance "to be a boy," as he put it. Together with his son
Kermit, he traveled to Brazil to the River of Doubt, a tributary

of the Amazon that had never been explored. When Roosevelt's party arrived at the river, the team of Brazilians that had accompanied them would travel no further. Leaving them behind, Roosevelt told the rest of the party to meet him at the other end of the river. Roosevelt's journey, which included impassable rapids, was considered one of the most dangerous of that time. Sixty day later, the former President emerged from the jungle, having shed fifty pounds. He had discovered the River of Doubt.

We can turn the place of doubt into a place that displays our name as a conqueror.

The famous Brazilian explorer Rondon gave the river a new name, the Rio Teodoro, after the president who conquered the River of Doubt. We too can turn the place of doubt into a place that displays our name as a conqueror in faith.

Sometimes, people have to journey on by themselves. We must provide the freedom that others need to continue their journey and to find their own way, remaining clear about our own responsibilities.

Remain faithful

It's important that we remember God's faithfulness when a mentor or a loved one leaves us alone.

Elijah was determined to put as much space between him and
Jezebel's militia as he possibly could. He had already outrun
Ahab's chariots, so he knew that he could outrun Jezebel's
henchmen. Elijah ran south, deep into the desolate wastes of
the Negev desert. In his haste, he had forgotten what his
servant lad remembered: that God is faithful.

Elijah ran for an entire day. He ran until his lungs nearly burst.
He ran even though his mouth grew parched from inhaling the
dry desert air. He ran until his powerful legs could carry him no
further. Spying a scrubby juniper tree, he stumbled toward it
and collapsed in its scraggly shade.

Like any desert nomad, Elijah knew that a man could survive
on the stringy roots of this desert tree. At this low point in his
prophetic career, however, Elijah wasn't even sure he wanted
to survive. In his divided emotions, he thought it might be
better to simply lie down and die. Why carry on? What good
had it done him to defy the forces of evil in the world? Nothing
had changed; the wicked were still in the place of power. Why
not simply ask God to put an end to his despondency? Elijah
had endured enough.

Even spiritual giants feel beaten at times. Even great heroes of
the faith have fallen into the ditch of despair. In this state of
utter despondency and dismay, utterly exhausted by his
exercise in self-preservation, Elijah fell asleep. The prophet

had completely forgotten that the same God who was with him when he defeated the prophets of Baal on Carmel was still with him under the juniper tree.

The mind is an amazing repository of memories. When Elijah and his young servant traveled together during happier days, they spent many hours exchanging stories of God's miracles and His faithfulness. These memories still nurtured the heart of Elijah's servant while his master was gone. Like this young man, when we are left alone, we can remind ourselves of how God has been faithful to us.

As Elijah went into the desert, he left behind more than his young servant. He left a portfolio of memories. Somehow, the amazing achievements and exciting experiences of his service to Yahweh had vanished from his view. In his despair and his despondency, Elijah had forgotten God. Elijah had an impressive list of Godly accomplishments that should have burned white hot in his remembrance.

If Elijah had begun taking inventory of these memories, he would have recalled:
- The announcement of the famine
- A raven that delivered his food
- The widow's barrel of flour that never emptied
- A woman's son brought from death to life
- A celestial fire that rained upon Carmel

- How rain returned in answer to his prayers
- The supernatural stamina that enabled him to outrun the king's chariot

Had Elijah focused on the same memories that sustained his servant, the embers of his faith could have been fanned to life. God's Holy Spirit could have encouraged him from these mighty acts. "Elijah you are not new to this," God could have whispered. "I was with you during these miracles. Remember Elijah — your God is faithful to His promises."

There is a reason that people in our country visit national monuments: these shrines remind them of their citizenship and help them to appreciate their freedoms. There is a reason people go to Washington to visit the Lincoln Memorial, visit the Tomb of the Unknown Soldier, the Vietnam War Memorial, and the Martin Luther King Jr. Center.

We can find victory over our doubts and emerge with our faith and our self-respect intact.

The National Archives house copies of the founding documents of our nation. Each night, these precious, irreplaceable documents mechanically sink into the caverns beneath the building to preserve them. Even when these monuments are locked up at night, we still have powerful memories that God has blessed us with. Our internal archives don't have visiting hours; they never shut down for holidays. Like Elijah's servant, we can visit these archives of God's faithfulness whenever we want.

Each of us has our personal archives. We should visit them. We should preserve our remembrance of the people, the places, the moments and the spaces where God met us and demonstrated His faithfulness. We each have memories that encourage us; it doesn't matter if those events seem insignificant to others. The important thing is that they remind us of God's faithfulness. Because of that, we should visit them to sustain our faith.

Trust in a caring God

When we are left alone, we have to trust our loved ones to the heart of a caring God. We must remember that our God is more than able to find them and to care for them. Even though the prodigal prophet ran, God pursued Elijah and came to him as he camped out under the juniper tree.

Like Elijah, most of us have our desert days of despair. There are days when we forget the faithfulness of our Lord. There are days when God seems remote and removed from our struggles. There are days when we have more pain than pleasure, days when life seems a relentless erosion of our stamina and our strength. There are days when we focus only on the futility and frustrations of the present, forgetting the unremitting faithfulness of God in the past.

When we see no hope or cheering prospect for the future, we are desperately in need of a touch from God. We need Christ's gracious spirit to reassure us of His willingness to sustain, encourage and refresh us.

God found Elijah beneath the juniper tree. He found him, **No matter how great the past, we cannot serve in the strength of past performance.** knowing that he was faint and desiring death. He found him, knowing that he was tired and thirsty. God found Elijah and cared tenderly for His famished prophet. He didn't rebuke Elijah. He didn't reprimand him for forgetting about His faithfulness. Instead God touched and revitalized Elijah. Knowing that he needed restoration from fatigue, God fed him. It's no easy thing to be called by God to single-handedly battle the forces of evil in a corrupt culture.

When the angel awakened Elijah a second time, he again encouraged him to eat and drink heartily. The angel knew that Elijah would need all of his strength to make the cross-country trip to Sinai. The trip, which was a minimum of 300 miles under terrifying temperatures, would bring Elijah back to the beginnings of Israel.

God was bringing Elijah to the same mountain where He had spoken to Moses amidst smoke, fire and dark clouds. He was

taking his prophet to the same cave where God had hidden
Moses when He passed by to show His glory.

In the cave, Elijah witnessed a violent wind so powerful that it
split a rock. The man of God was shaken by an earthquake and
saw the flash of flames. Elijah searched, but God was not in
the wind, in the earthquake, or in the fire. God came to him on
the soft whisper of a breeze. As He spoke to the prophet, the
voice of God was unmistakable. Twice God asked Elijah,
"Why are you here?"

When Elijah was alone with God, he returned to the place
where he began. He came back to his starting point, needing to
hear a word from God. There is a tremendous truth here for us:
No matter how great the past, we cannot serve in the strength
of past performance. We cannot hope to be sustained only by
our past experience. We cannot live today on last week's food.
Like the children of Israel, each morning we must find fresh
manna to nourish us for today's work.

God found Elijah and cared for him when he was vulnerable
beneath a tree. God found Elijah and spoke to him when he
was hiding in the cave. Regardless of where our loved ones
run, God is looking for them, seeking to restore them, just as
did with Elijah.

When we are running from God, He will find us too. When

we're lying exposed beneath the juniper tree of despondency, God can find us and care for us. When we're hiding in the cave of despair, God can touch us and speak to us there.

When one of these life-changing encounters happened to one pastor near Burleson, Texas, it created a memorable moment in American church history.

Dr. George W. Truett, the legendary pastor of the First Baptist Church of Dallas, had gone on a hunting trip with his friend Captain Arnold, chief of the Dallas police department. Truett carelessly handled his weapon while crossing a barbed wire fence, discharging the lead birdshot into his friend's leg. Arnold dismissed the injury and the party caught a train back to Dallas.

Truett, however, couldn't shake the sense of foreboding. Three

When we are left alone, we have to trust our loved ones to the heart of a caring God.

days later, Arnold was dead. Crazed, delirious, and inconsolable, Truett locked himself in his Dallas home. Everyone thought his ministerial career was over, that he would never preach again. An encounter with the Savior changed that. One night, Jesus came to Arnold three times in three separate dreams. Each time, the Lord told him, "George, you are my man now."

Truett returned to the church on the following Sunday evening. The crowds thronged the historic sanctuary and Arnold's ministry knew a power and an anointing like never before. Even though our situation may not be as dramatic as Truett's, our God is still the same.

We must not be surprised when God asks, "Why are you here?" In His great love, He wants to restore us and move us away from the places where we run to hide.

Prepare to welcome them back
When we're left alone by a loved one, we must be ready to welcome them home. We must also be ready to rejoin them in a new assignment.

Elijah's servant had been waiting and praying for his spiritual leader. He wasn't aware that God had reassigned Elijah and given him a new commission. Elijah was now charged with anointing the new king of Syria. God was using the prophet to bring a new royal dynasty into this foreign nation.

Regardless of how lost he'd been, Elijah had rediscovered his compass and it was pointing him northward. God had always been Elijah's compass; when God found the prophet in the cave, He pointed him in the right direction again.

I have a friend who keeps a compass for camping trips with his sons. Since they camp only once a year, the compass often gets misplaced along with other camping gear. Sometimes, it's in a

When we take our doubts to the Lord, we make Him Lord over our doubts. sack, sometimes in a drawer, sometimes in a storage room and sometimes carelessly left on the third shelf in the laundry. Despite where he finds it, my friend noted a simple but striking fact: Every time he finds the compass, it is still pointing north. We may rest assured of the same truth in the spiritual realm. Wherever and whenever someone loses the way, God's compass always points them in the right direction.

When those we love return, restored by God, we should also expect things to be a bit different. We should expect them to return with a new assignment. We should expect to join them as we walk together with God, headed in the right direction. We must be ready.

There was another man who walked into the wilderness. When the Son of God emerged from those barren places, He walked out with words that would never be bestowed on anyone else, the assurance that He was the Suffering Servant Substitute. Our great High Priest walked in and then walked out of the desert of doubt. When He walked out, the evangelist, Luke, reminds us that He walked out full of the Holy Ghost and power.

It's only our Great Shepherd who can lead us out of this

solitary place, out of this place where we're left alone. Only He can lead His sheep out of the wilderness. Only He can speak the words that our souls need to hear.

Jesus walked out of the desert and on to Nazareth; He went to speak the words the Father had given Him. He met the deceiver on Satan's own turf and bound him there. In victory over doubt and temptation, our Lord walked into Nazareth and destiny, never to taste such doubt until He struggled with the will of the Father in Gethsemane. Even

When we put our despair under His dominion, He will destroy despair.

there, He walked out in triumph and in victory. He went with the Spirit of the Lord upon Him; He went anointed to preach the gospel to the lost. He went to those left alone in a desert of doubt.

Like Elijah, we sometimes run away. But if we know Him, we are always running toward Him. When Elijah sat under the tree, it cast a shadow that protected him in the desert. We sit under a tree that casts its shadow across the ages — a tree called Calvary. Elijah found God again on the mount called Sinai; we find God again on the mount called Golgotha.

When we take our doubts to the Lord, we make Him Lord over our doubts. That's when our doubts begin to die, our discouragement disappears, and our despair diminishes. When we take our discouragement to the Savior, He saves us from discouragement. When we put our despair under His dominion, He will destroy despair.

Reflection Questions

Suggested readings: 1 Kings 19 and Hebrews 11:32-40

1. Has someone close to you not allowed you to come along on his or her personal journey into the wilderness? Did you struggle to release them? How might you have handled the situation differently?

2. How do you tend to handle doubt during trying experiences? For example, do you turn to behaviors that helped you cope in the past? Have you found ways to respond faithfully?

3. What memories of God's faithfulness in your life can you assemble into a personal archive to help you deal with times of discouragement?

4. How easy or difficult is it for you to make Jesus the Lord of your doubts? How might you improve in this area? What specific areas can you deal with now?

If we had no winter, the spring would not be so pleasant; if we did not sometimes taste of adversity, prosperity would not be so welcome.

— Anne Bradstreet

Faith is the first factor in a life devoted to service. Without it, nothing is possible. With it, nothing is impossible.

— Mary McLeod Bethune

Chapter Four — No Longer Left Alone
John 14:15-18

General Douglas MacArthur forged a bond with the people of the Philippine Islands during World War II. Throughout the conflict, he promised them his loyalty. The general kept his word, remaining with them at the risk of his life, staying on even when Japanese forces attacked the islands heavily.

President Franklin Roosevelt ordered MacArthur to leave the Philippines in 1942. Against his wishes, the general packed, gathered his family and got into a boat to make his way to Australia. Before he departed, he made the famous statement, "I shall return." MacArthur also kept that promise. In 1944, he returned and freed the Philippines from Japanese control. During his absence, reminders of his promised return were everywhere. The islanders wrote his now-famous words on their sandy beaches, carved them into coconuts and printed them on matchbook covers.

Our world will one day witness a return that promises to be infinitely more satisfying than General MacArthur's. During the last week of His public ministry, Jesus spoke frequently of His own return. "I go to prepare a place for you. And if I go and prepare a place for you, I will come again and receive you to Myself; that where I am, there you may be also."[1] Jesus also

told His disciples that He will not leave them alone. He said
that His followers won't be treated like orphans. Because Jesus
keeps His promises, those words are just as comforting and
inspiring for us today as they were for the disciples who
walked with our Lord two thousand years ago.

Today, Jesus is even more present than He was when he walked
with His disciples in Galilee. The
famous Baptist Greek scholar, A.T.
Robertson, was convinced of this.
He opened his monumental book on
grammar by assuring his readers that
the Christ we meet on the pages of
the New Testament is more alive today that He was in the days
of His flesh.

**When we're hiding
in the cave of
despair, God can
touch us and
speak to us there.**

When our hearts are troubled, when we're weighed down by
life, when we're struggling with anxiety, our humanity longs to
be close to God. During those times, having Jesus near is a
soothing balm. When I feel like I've been left alone, when I feel
like no one understands my troubles and my circumstances, the
words of Jesus in John 14 remind me that I'm still in God's
presence. It's reassuring for me to know that He promises to
never leave or forsake me.

Look at these promises from Jesus. Hear anew how our Lord
comes to the weak. Hear again about the promised Holy Spirit.

Hear how His strength and power can give the energy that we so desperately need to face the difficulties of this life. Let's examine John 14:15-18.

"If you love me, keep my commandments. And I will pray the Father, and he shall give you another helper that he may abide with you forever. The Spirit of truth, whom the world cannot receive, because it neither sees him nor knows him, but you know him for he dwells with you and will be in you. I will not leave you orphans. I will come to you."

These words are the farewell discourse of Jesus to His disciples. The disciples had grown accustomed to Jesus being with them. As He began speaking to them as described in John 14, their hearts were breaking because they now understood that He was leaving. When they heard these words, the contours of their faces shifted, their expressions changed, and their hearts were saddened by the possibility of His absence. Jesus takes this opportunity to remind them that He cannot be everywhere and with everyone. He explains that it is expedient for Him to leave so that He can expand His presence and be with everyone, everywhere, at the same time.

Imagine if Jesus had said, "I'm going to Jerusalem." Every time we wanted to communicate with Him, we'd have to take a trans-Atlantic flight. We'd have to travel to Tel Aviv, go to the Holy Land, find Jesus and get an appointment. Thankfully, Jesus didn't go to Jerusalem. He returned to the Father so that He's available in a manner that enables Him to be everywhere at the same time. It means that He can be with me in Houston, with brothers in New York, sisters in California, churches in South America, in Europe, and in Africa at the same time. There's no loss of His presence; it's not like spotty cell phone coverage. Jesus is available everywhere with the same dynamic presence.

People who want to pay homage to the memory of Napoleon can go to Paris and visit the cathedral that has his wonderful casket. People who wish to see the sarcophagus of the Duke of Wellington will go to St. Paul's Church in England. Patriots interested in the lives of past presidents might travel to

When we take our discouragement to the Savior, He saves us from discouragement.

Springfield, Illinois and visit the tomb of Abraham Lincoln. Those who want to remember civil rights leaders go to Atlanta to the tomb of Martin Luther King, Jr. But when we want to worship Jesus, we don't need to travel long distances. Because of the Holy Spirit, Jesus is with us right now. That's why Jesus had to leave; He had to stop being *somewhere* so that He could be *everywhere*. The legacy of His promise is the ever-present Holy Spirit, the universal presence of Christ.

Jesus kept this promise. Had Jesus not kept His promise to send the Spirit, the early church would have died in the womb.

Regardless of how long they continued waiting, nothing would have happened.

When the famous magician Harry Houdini died in 1926, he left a ten-word message with his wife Bess. He ordered a trust fund to pay anyone who could receive a communication from him in the life beyond that matched those ten words. Despite Houdini's promise that he would try to make contact from beyond the grave, no one legitimately completed this challenge.

Our Lord Jesus Christ is no heavenly Houdini. He promised to send a message — the Comforter — and that message arrived, just as He promised. If Jesus had not sent that message, there would have been no Pentecost, no Church and no Christianity. Peter would have returned to his nets and Matthew would have resumed his career with Rome's version of the Internal Revenue Service.

Many Christians seem to be misinformed about the basics of the Holy Spirit; they seemed to have skipped this portion of Christianity 101. Too many have only heard others talk about the Holy Spirit without taking the time to really examine what Scripture says. When they do hear about the Holy Spirit, it's from someone who gives too much inaccurate information. They hear people saying that the Holy Ghost got them clapping, running and shouting. Unfortunately, there are plenty of other things that can make you behave that way.

When Jesus says the Father will send "another helper," the
words that He used tell us how this helper comes and what He
does. Let's look more closely at some of the words that
Scripture uses to describe the Holy Spirit.

In John 14, Jesus says that He will ask the Father to give us
another helper. In the Greek New Testament, those words —
allon parakleton — mean "one of the same kind." Jesus doesn't
use the words *heteros parakleton*, which would mean "of
another kind." He specifically chooses words to communicate
that the helper, the paraclete that He sends will be like Him.

Here's what Jesus was saying. "I will ask the Father to give
you another, someone who is exactly the same as I am. In my
absence, this helper will be for you what I've been when I was
present. The Holy Spirit will be what I was when we were
together at the Sea of Galilee, in the city of Capernaum, and in
Jerusalem. Whatever I did, the Holy Spirit will continue to do.
Even though I'm going away, you will not lose anything that
you experienced when I was present."

In some translations, this verse — John 14:16 — refers to the
Holy Spirit as *another comforter.* Don't mistake the word
"comforter" to be something passive. In its English origin, this
word reflects the combination *con fortis*, which means "with
strength." In our English nomenclature, *comfort* suggests

something that's weak, romantic, fuzzy and soft. But the original language uses a military term that carries the notion of support and strength. In that context, "comfort" means that when our hearts are troubled, when we are weak and beside ourselves, He will come alongside to provide support. He will lay His hands on our shoulders, providing us with strength and power. He's going to tell us that He's walking with us through our valleys, through the shadow of death and through disappointment.

Sometimes, the Holy Spirit is described as *another advocate.* John writes that, "We have a mediator between God and man, an advocate that makes intercession for us."[2] He also implies that this one who is to come, the Holy Spirit, will plead on

Because of the Holy Spirit, Jesus is with us right now.

our behalf. He will plead our case before the cosmic courts. We have somebody who will represent us, a heavenly advocate.

In some places, the Holy Spirit is *another counselor.* John 14:26 tells us that as a counselor, the Holy Spirit will teach us all things and remind us of everything that Jesus said. When we're confused, He'll straighten us out; He will be our counselor. The Father provided *another*, one who is just like Jesus in every way.

There are many fascinating stories about twins and identical twins. None of them capture the imagination like the story of the "Jim twins." After their biological mother put them up for adoption, these two identical twin boys were sent to different homes and separated for 39 years. After years of searching, the brothers found each other.

Jim Lewis said that meeting his identical twin brother, Jim Springer, was like looking in a mirror. Although they'd been apart for nearly four decades, they discovered an enormous number of similarities. Both Jims:

- Had been adopted by families from Ohio
- Were named "Jim" by their adoptive parents and named a dog "Toy" when they were boys
- Suffered from migraine headaches, were fretful sleepers and nail biters.
- Married twice. Their first wives were both named Linda; their second wives were both named Betty
- Had sons. One was named "Jim Allen;" the other was Jim Alan
- Smoked Salem cigarettes, drank Miller Lite beer, loved stock car racing and hated baseball
- Built children's furniture in the basement and constructed circular white benches around the trees in their backyards
- Had the same IQ, nearly the same heartbeat pattern, brainwaves and almost identical handwriting
- Died on the same day

The Jim twins are an astounding example of how two people can be nearly identical in every way and yet retain discrete identities. Jesus Christ of Nazareth and the Holy Spirit are two discrete Persons in the Holy Trinity, yet they are the one and the same. Their mission is the same, their personality is the same and their power is the same.

When Jesus said, "one of the same kind," He meant that He and the Holy Spirit were even more identical than the Jim twins. There's absolutely no difference between them. Everything that Jesus did, the Holy Spirit is doing.

When the great preacher Charles Spurgeon died in 1892, his church tried to rekindle his spirit in their midst. In their sad longing, they had his brother, his son and his close associates serve as pastor. While his followers tried and tried to find someone to occupy the empty space that this great Christian preacher had in their hearts, it never happened. Never again would they experience that connection. Only Jesus can send His presence and His spirit to us from the life beyond.

Had Jesus not kept His promise to send the Spirit, the early church would have died in the womb.

I want to encourage you to increase your appreciation of the person and the presence of the Holy Spirit. Have you considered that without the Holy Spirit, we cannot witness and we cannot know the truth? Scripture says that He's the one who guides us. He's our counselor, our teacher, and the one who instructs us. We need the power of the Holy Spirit to be functional believers. Take some time to thoroughly examine what Scripture says about Him.

Scripture makes it clear that Jesus now comes to us in a more powerful and dynamic way than He ever did in the past. "The Spirit of truth, whom the world cannot receive, because it neither sees him nor knows him, but you know him for he dwells with you and will be in you." (John 15:17)

Up until this moment, the God of the Old Testament had been with Israel, dwelling in clouds, in tabernacles and temples, and in the Ark of the Covenant. Yahweh had been with them in budding rods, He had been with them in stone tablets and He had come to them through sacrificial offerings and covenant regulations. But when Jesus Christ came, the God who was far off came near. The Word became flesh and dwelt among us.

When Jesus told His disciples that He was about to leave, He also explained how much closer He would dwell. He said, "I will not leave you alone. I will give you another just like me — the spirit of truth. You will know him because you have known me. He will be **with** you — but also _in_ you."

Jesus had been with His disciples on multiple occasions and

they had seen Him demonstrate His power. Today, He wants the church to know that because the Holy Spirit came, Jesus has established residence inside of us. Jesus is with us in the same way that He had been with His disciples in the past.

We shouldn't be astonished when we hear of God working miracles today. It shouldn't baffle our minds. The same Jesus who worked miracles in Galilee is the same Savior who is performing them today. In fact, Scripture says that we will do greater works than those done in the past. We ought to be witnessing something more dynamic and different because the Holy Spirit lives within us. If the church really believed that, we wouldn't be able to build buildings large enough to contain the multitudes that would come.

In addition to being **with** us, Jesus says that He's also *in* us. He has become part of our very essence. He uses our hands and our feet, our minds and our mouths. That's what Paul spoke about in Galatians. He said, "I'm a new man in Christ — Christ is in me. And now the life that I live is no longer mine. It's the life of Christ, who's in me."[3]

Because the truth of God is available to everyone, Christians are not the only ones who believe that Christ is still present today. An interviewer once asked Albert Einstein his thoughts on Jesus, wondering what this great mind thought about people who claimed that Jesus was the Christ. Standing in his laboratory, Einstein said, "Anyone who reads the New Testament and meets Jesus on its pages leaves understanding he's more real in this laboratory than he was 2,000 years ago."

"I will not leave you orphans. I will come to you." The word "orphans" that Jesus uses here in John 15:18 is only used in one other place, which is James 1:27. Scholars have not given a strict definition of what that word means. It's safe to assume that it's saying that we won't be left fatherless.

Since fathers provide resources, this verse communicates that God will provide whatever we need when the Holy Spirit comes to us. As you're reading this, pause and ask yourself what you need from God. I'm not talking about some cheap trinkets. I'm not talking about cars, adding more square footage to your house, or fancy designer clothes. The things that we need from God are those things that money cannot buy.

What we need is peace. The peace that the Holy Spirit brings — the "shalom" of God — is what miraculously puts us back together when we're falling apart. We also need joy, which many people confuse with happiness. Happiness is situational: we're happy that we have a job or companionship. But if you need someone or something to make you happy, that's not joy. Joy comes from abiding with God; it's in His presence that we find fullness of joy.

Sometimes, it is good to be left alone. It might not appear that way initially, but in hindsight, we can see how it benefits us. In John 16:7-8, Jesus explained to His disciples how His leaving would help them. "But I tell you the truth: It is for your good that I am going away. Unless I go away, the Counselor will not come to you; but if I go, I will send him to you."

Jesus wasn't going away to bring sadness upon His followers; He was leaving so that they would never be alone again. He would dwell within them, walking even closer and in a much more dynamic way.

Our Lord tried to tell the disciples about the Holy Spirit, but they didn't quite get it. They scratched their heads when Jesus said, "In a little while you will see me no more, and then after a little while you will see me." They wouldn't understand what Jesus was talking about until Pentecost.

The very essence of the Christian experience shouts that Jesus hasn't left us alone. "Christ in you," writes Paul, "the hope of Glory."[4]

Because God dwells closer than ever before, because He lives within us through the Holy Spirit, we truly are no longer alone.

References
1. John 14:2b-3
2. 1 John 2:1
3. Galatians 2:20
4. Colossians 1:27

Reflection Questions

Suggested readings: John 14:15-18 and Romans 8 (entire chapter)

1. Is it difficult for you to believe that Jesus is as alive and present with you today as He was when He walked the earth?

2. Recall your first encounter with the Holy Spirit. List the changes the Holy Spirit has made in your life.

3. In what ways might God be encouraging you to experience Christ's comforting presence through the Holy Spirit?

Conclusion

You can be sure that every life is often clouded by mysteries, impossibilities and uncertainties. No one is exempt.

Even our Savior wrestled with what seemed like incongruous events in His life, causing Him to weep, to sweat drops of blood and to cry out, "My God, my God! Why have you forsaken Me?" When we encounter troubling times, we can take comfort in the knowledge that we are walking in the steps of our Great High Priest.

As much as we might not want to see these problems appearing on our doorsteps, they are as inevitable as the rain that falls on the just and on the unjust. As Job expresses so clearly, "Man is born to trouble, as the sparks fly upward."[1]

In these pages, we've journeyed over the less frequently traveled back roads of trials and tribulations. As I've paused to view these Biblical stories in a broader perspective in my life, it's become clear to me that it's not the events that are important — it's our response to them that makes the difference.

In the final analysis, what we choose to do with life's mysteries, impossibilities and uncertainties will shape our character. By recognizing that we have the constant support of the Holy Spirit, we cooperate with God in transforming an impossible, trying circumstance into a destiny shaped by Heaven.

This path we walk is not an easy one. Our struggles may not even be comprehensible to our limited mortal minds and hearts. But we are not on a solitary journey. We have a Brother born to provide comfort in adversity and a Friend who sticks closer than a brother. With that, we can be content.

References
1. Job 5:7

About Ralph Douglas West

Ralph Douglas West is the pastor and founder of The Church Without Walls, Houston, Texas.

He is the author of *Finding Fullness Again: What the Book of Ruth Teaches Us About Starting Over*, (B&H Publishing, May 2006) and co-author of *Preaching Evangelistically: Proclaiming the Saving Message of Jesus* (B&H Publishing, May 2005).

In 1987, Dr. West founded Brookhollow Baptist Church. Under his leadership, the congregation grew from 32 members to well over 19,000 members and was transformed into The Church Without Walls. The church now ministers to more than 14,000 families in three locations.

He is married to Sheretta Machell Grays West and has two sons, Ralph Douglas II and Ralpheal Daniel.

Also by Ralph Douglas West

Finding Fullness Again: What the Book of Ruth Teaches Us About Starting Over

There are times when every believer arrives at a desolate place, where their hearts or spirits are crushed. *Finding Fullness Again* takes an encouraging look at the story of Naomi and Ruth to remind readers that they too can keep pressing forward — despite the weight of their cares. (B&H Publishing, May 2006).

Preaching Evangelistically: Proclaiming the Saving Message of Jesus *(co-author)*

It's easy to forget the purpose of preaching: to proclaim God's salvation through Jesus. *Preaching Evangelistically* looks at the different elements of gospel preaching and how they can effectively proclaim Jesus. (B&H Publishing, May 2005).

For more information or to order copies:
- Visit **www.ralphdouglaswest.org**
- Call **1-888-377-6876**